Middle East Negotiations

A Conversation with Joseph Sisco

Middle East Negotiations

A Conversation with Joseph Sisco

With Basic Documents

Held on June 9, 1980
at the American Enterprise Institute for Public Policy Research
Washington, D.C.

ISBN 0-8447-3394-6

Library of Congress Catalog Card No. 80-68757

AEI Studies 289

Printed in the United States of America

Foreword

This discussion is another in a series of "Conversations" sponsored by AEI with outstanding public figures—in and out of government—and with scholars and specialists who have made noteworthy contributions to the formation of public policy. Since the series was launched in 1975, we have invited to AEI, among others, Senator Richard G. Lugar and Senator Daniel Patrick Moynihan, Lane Kirkland of the AFL-CIO, Secretary of Labor Ray Marshall, Robert Strauss, Gerald Ford, the Reverend Jesse Jackson, Philip Crane, John Connally, and Mayor Marion Barry of Washington, D.C. The format for these conversations —a brief presentation, followed by discussion with members of a limited audience of AEI scholars and guests—is intended to produce a minimum of "talking at" the audience and a maximum of speaking to, and listening to, each other.

This booklet is a transcript of an AEI "Conversation," edited, as lightly as possible, to preserve the informal conversational nature of the discussion. We believe that this sort of exchange offers a perspective on the thinking of important public figures very different from that found in their prepared speeches and published writings. And, we believe, it is an excellent way to encourage the "competition of ideas" that is AEI's trademark.

WILLIAM J. BAROODY, JR.
President
American Enterprise Institute
for Public Policy Research

Introductory Remarks

Robert A. Goldwin
AEI Resident Scholar

Joseph Sisco is one of this country's truly professional, high-level diplomats. He is experienced, knowledgeable, and expert. He received his Ph.D. in international relations from the University of Chicago in 1950. As undersecretary of state for political affairs, Mr. Sisco held the top career post in the foreign service. He has also been president of American University and is currently its chancellor.

But for our subject today, the most relevant facts are these: from 1965 to 1969 Dr. Sisco was assistant secretary of state for international organization affairs; in 1967 he was the U.S. representative to the fifth special session of the United Nations General Assembly on the Middle East; and from 1969 to 1974 he was assistant secretary for Near Eastern and South Asian affairs and the U.S. negotiator on the Arab-Israeli settlement—in short, the principal adviser on Middle Eastern issues. When the subject is UN Resolution 242 and all related issues of the Middle East, Joseph Sisco is an indispensable national resource. He is our most authoritative living memory bank, the man who was there and who played a major role in the most significant actions and decisions.

Middle East Negotiations: A Conversation with Joseph Sisco

The timing of this conversation is rather good, because a major effort is being made to reopen the autonomy talks in the Middle East—although I don't believe they are the central feature of developments in that area at the present time, as important as they are. Regardless of the difficulties with the autonomy talks since the conclusion of the Egyptian-Israeli Treaty, these discussions may result in a limited success (and I will define limited success in a moment) by the end of 1980. The Egyptian-Israeli Treaty itself represents the most far-reaching step forward in the history of the Arab-Israeli dispute. When we consider that the last three decades have been punctuated by four wars, that during at least two of these decades there were no negotiations or contact whatsoever, but that in the latter half of the 1970s two disengagement agreements—between Egypt and Israel and between Syria and Israel—were effected and when we look at the subsequent Camp David agreements and the Egyptian-Israeli Treaty, we have to conclude that substantial progress has been made.

To be provocative, I throw out this idea: perhaps, as a result of developments over the last five to seven years, the peace process in the Middle East has become irreversible. Some, no doubt, will challenge this proposition. But the Egyptian-Israeli Treaty has fundamentally altered the military balance in the Middle East. War will not be a viable Arab option in the foreseeable future as long as Anwar Sadat and Egypt remain within the peace process. Syria's President Hafez Assad has severely criticized President Sadat for obtaining a "separate" treaty between Egypt and Israel, because he knows that a one-front war against Israel would not be a viable option even if Syria were to develop a broad support in other parts of the Arab world, particularly among the more radical elements.

Now if this assessment of the progress of peace is correct, it is no reason for any of us to relax or to believe for a moment that the current violence and counterviolence by extremists on both sides, particularly in the West Bank, will not lead to a very serious situation in the future. These activities have risen out of continuing frustration, out of reaction to the settlements policy of the Begin government, and out of the continuing desire, both of the Palestinians and the Palestinian Liberation Organization (PLO) to remain part of the act. Between now and the end of the year, while these talks go on—and they will undoubtedly resume—we may see much more such violence, but perhaps it will not get out of control. No one can be relaxed about that situation, but I don't believe that the activities of extremists will necessarily impact on the autonomy talks over the next six months for one simple reason: both Menachem Begin and Sadat want to avoid a breakdown.

Moreover, the limited success that may be possible here is very limited indeed. At best, we can expect an agreement that really sets aside many of the critical issues of water, land, and security, and that simply focuses on the establishment of an instrumentality of autonomy or of self-government. Such an instrumentality would not try to define too precisely what the responsibilities of the governing council for the West Bank would be. Somehow, it will skate between the view of Sadat, who wants autonomy to be defined fully, down to executive and legislative responsibilities, and that of Begin, who, despite the words "full autonomy" in the Camp David accords, seeks a type of autonomy that is limited largely to municipal, administrative, and day-to-day nonpolitical activities that would preclude an opportunity for the eventual creation of a Palestinian state.

Some other factors are affecting these talks, in addition to the increase in violence in the West Bank. The political dynamics in Israel itself have become very important. First, there is increasing concern over the continuation of the actual occupation. A visitor to Israel will find that, no matter what the political stripe, the substantial majority of the people want an end to the occupation of the West Bank and the Gaza, feeling that this has become more and more onerous. The occupation, of course, should be terminated, but not without measures assuring Israel's security. This is absolutely vital: I can't conceive of any kind of agreement, on an interim basis or otherwise, that would, in Israeli eyes, undermine their need for both long-range and short-range security.

A second part of the political dynamic in Israel is the increasing disagreement within the body politic over the shape of the ultimate solution for the West Bank. Begin has talked about autonomy for the people. He may have in mind integrating the West Bank and the Gaza within the broad framework of a unified Israeli state. This possibility raises fundamental concerns about which Aba Eban has been the most eloquent—namely, that if the ultimate solution envisaged by Begin were applied it would bring a million Arabs inside the borders of the state of Israel and would jeopardize its Jewish character. The Labor party, on the other hand, has supported the notion of an interim agreement in accordance with the second half of the Camp David accord, but only as a step toward a territorial solution in the West Bank.

I, for one, believe that the solution in the West Bank and Gaza has to be territorial. That means that at some point King Hussein of Jordan will have to be brought into the process. At some point there will have to be a division of territory whereby Jews will be living within a state of Israel and that part of the territory returned to the Arabs will be within the Arab world itself. Such questions about how the Palestinian problem will be resolved are extremely important, because obviously there cannot be either peace or stability without resolving the Palestinian issue.

One final element of the Israeli political dynamic: I feel that Begin will hang on, that there will not be an early election for this reason, and that, although Dayan and Weizman resigned, neither carried enough weight in the Knesset for their supporters to bring down the Begin government. Therefore, the delicate balance that Begin is maintaining by retaining the defense portfolio himself will probably continue.

Another reason to suppose that the Begin government will remain in power for some time is that the Labor party is divided. A year ago there was absolutely no doubt that Peres was the heir apparent and the titular head of the Labor party, but in the last six to eight weeks two polls conducted within Israel surprisingly have indicated a major resurgence of Prime Minister Rabin, who leads Peres by eight to ten points. This means that, if elections are held in 1981, the division within the Labor party will have had enough time to develop into a bloodier battle than anyone would have predicted a year ago, when Peres faced no serious challenge. Remember that, under Israel's constitution, even if there were an election the incumbent would become the caretaker, so that Begin could conceivably be in power as a caretaker for at least four or five months. So for all practical purposes we will be dealing with a Begin government between now and our November election, and it will be what he says and what he does with respect to the autonomy talks that determine whether they succeed or fail.

As for other parts of the Arab world, Hussein will probably not enter into these talks for two principal reasons. First, he wants to see what the light is at the end of the tunnel; obviously there have been no indications of any major breakthrough from a territorial point of view to make these talks attractive to King Hussein. Second, and I would like to be very blunt about this, we must remember that regardless of King Hussein's reservation, the present status quo between Israel and Jordan is not altogether unsatisfactory to Hussein. Over the years Israel and Jordan have cooperated on a de facto basis in keeping raids and perpetrators of violence out of the West Bank. In the long run, Jordan and Israel have one thing in common: whatever solution is reached with respect to the West Bank and the Gaza, both sides will have to live with it. Hussein knows very well that if the solution found becomes a threat to him, that Palestinian guns could as readily be pointed eastward at Hussein as westward at Israel. Many of us tend to forget that in the long run Jordan and Israel have these parallel, if not common, interests. That was one of the reasons that, while I was at the State Department, we tried to convince our Israeli friends to put forward the kinds of proposals that would have been attractive to Hussein.

Turning now to UN Resolution 242, several interpretations of this important resolution have been put forth. At the time that Security Council Resolution 242 was passed, the Arab side and the Soviet side took it to mean total Israeli withdrawal to the lines that existed before June 1967. Our interpretation was and is that the resolution calls for "secure and recognized boundaries," which is a phrase that was put together by a number of people behind the scenes. The resolution neither endorses nor precludes—and that is key—the 1967 borders as the final borders in any ultimate solution. Interestingly, according to the Egyptian-Israeli Treaty the withdrawal that will be completed within two years is a withdrawal to the 1967 borders. I recall an earlier plan—the Rogers Plan—that called for withdrawal to those particular borders. It was said to be unacceptable then, but I am very very glad to see that it has been incorporated in the Egyptian-Israeli Treaty.

One of Sadat's reasons for not cutting off categorically the autonomy talks is that under the Camp David accord and under the Egyptian-Israeli Treaty, total Israeli withdrawal will not be completed until 1982. Without doubt, that is Sadat's primary objective. A second factor to consider is the recent evolution in the Arab world.

We cannot call it an accommodation, but at least the Arabs are living with the fact that Camp David was achieved, and with the permanency of the Egyptian-Israeli Treaty. Also important is the Saudi position, which is not necessarily a concern over the Egyptian-Israeli Treaty per se but a concern that it be a first step toward an overall settlement and not the last step and a separate agreement as such.

Certain newspapers have given undue attention to the recent Saudi statement that it would want to help in the peace process, subject of course to the same two conditions (understandable from their point of view), namely, total Israeli withdrawal and the achievement of a Palestinian solution. It is not insignificant that Saudi Arabia would say something along those lines, but there was an immediate pullback on that particular statement because obviously the last thing that the Saudis have wanted to do in the past or want to do in the future is to get out in front on this particular issue, even though they are in the best position in the Arab world to play a positive role. But their role has been and will continue to be behind the scenes.

We can summarize the general situation in this way: (1) Although we should be concerned about the violence and the counterviolence, which will surely continue throughout 1980, this probably will not mushroom into another all-out war between the Arabs and the Israelis in the foreseeable future. (2) As normalization and the implementation of the Egyptian-Israeli Treaty continue, the autonomy talks will probably limp along with limited success, perhaps in the form of a paper accord between Sadat and Begin permitting limited autonomy. Such an agreement would not soon attract Palestinian or Jordanian participation.

My concern about the violence and the counterviolence on the West Bank is that it might make radicals out of the moderate elements there. There are Palestinian leaders in the West Bank and the Gaza who do not necessarily support the PLO position, even though recent developments obviously make it difficult for Palestinians to take any political position other than that expressed by the PLO.

The significance of the recent meetings of the PLO hierarchy in Cairo is that they have tried to square the circle. They enunciated a so-called new policy of militancy, which was probably directed largely at various Arab audiences and certainly the political supporters of that view within the Arab world. During the second half of that meeting, the PLO reaffirmed the basic notion that they are continuing to seek a "political" solution. This part of their communiqué appeared to be directed at public opinion in the United States and particularly in Western Europe, which has developed an initiative on the Middle East situation. That initiative will be limited, at least between now and November, to a declaration, rather than an attempt at amending Security Council Resolution 242 in the UN Security Council. They will be deterred by the administration's announcement that any such attempt would be vetoed by the United States, and rightly so, in my judgment.

MR. GOLDWIN: We are ready now for the audience to participate in the conversation.

ROBERT PRANGER, American Enterprise Institute: You have had probably more experience than anyone in Washington in dealing with Israeli foreign policy decision making. Could you share some thoughts about the difficulties of getting a decision out of Israel on these issues?

MR. SISCO: One of the best ways to do this is to cite some concrete experiences and also to compare Israeli decision making with the process on the other side. In Cairo, Sadat is the number one force; and throughout the disengagement agreements and likewise throughout the Camp David negotiations, Sadat made the broad strategic decisions, leaving most of the specific details to his staff and his foreign ministers. At Camp David, of course, there were specific issues to discuss and with the President there, it was necessary for Sadat to focus more than he normally does on some of the details that needed to be resolved in order to achieve success. Generally, however, he first makes broad strategic decisions and then decides what concrete action to take on some of the tactical issues on the basis of whatever staff advice he gets. Sadat will probably have a fairly relaxed attitude in the current talks with respect to the nature of the autonomy instrumentality, because I think he probably attributes more importance to the actual ongoing process and to the establishment of some form of mechanism. He assigns overriding importance to that process, rather than to dotting every "i" or to trying to detail this autonomy agreement with specific elements on water or land settlements, and the functions of the governing council. If there is limited success, he will probably be willing to let some of these specific duties of the council be negotiated by the council on a de facto basis with the Israeli authorities. Of course some critical questions—such as where the power comes from, that is, whether it comes from the

Israeli authority or elsewhere—will have to be resolved before this kind of council can be established.

As for the process in Israel, we have to remember that there it is the democratic process in the most open sense. In order to keep up on developments on this issue from an Israeli point of view and to keep ahead by ten days of the American press, all one has to do is read the *Jerusalem Post* every day. Everything is leaked to the press in Israel, and apparently it doesn't make any difference what the stringencies are, what the instructions are—it just isn't possible, when a couple of handfuls of cabinet members are involved, to keep anything very quiet.

Mrs. Golda Meir once reminded me that when you've got five Jews in the room you've got ten points of view, and I mean this quite kindly and not in any derogatory sense. There is no doubt that Israel has a very open process. People who think the U.S. process is open should live in Israel about six months; they would soon realize that in Israel there are no secrets whatsoever.

Moreover, we cannot disregard the effect of the political coalition in Israel today, which is a delicate balance between the National Religious party and Yadin's Democratic party. Begin has no more than sixty-three votes in the 120-member Knesset. All that he would have to do is lose about three or four votes and the government would come down. And so he is involved in every decision, and every member of Begin's cabinet has to have his say. For that reason, a negotiator does not have any substantial latitude or any substantial freedom. Mr. Yosef Burg, who is the leader of the Israeli delegation, does not operate under a broad overall strategic umbrella, but every step of the way has to be checked tactically with the government back home. In fact, those possible steps become the subject of cabinet decisions and cabinet discussion on successive Sundays.

I remember an amusing incident in our negotiation for thirty-three consecutive days of the Syrian-Israeli disengagement agreement. Israel—a small state surrounded by a number of others—obviously, but understandably, had negotiated every minute step, every inch of territory, every tree, and so on. By contrast, in the Sinai Sadat had taken broad strategic decisions. But our difficulty in the Syrian-Israeli disengagement agreement was that the Syrians tended to negotiate like the Israelis. We were operating within a much more limited geographical confine than in the Sinai. We were also negotiating in a much more sensitive area from the point of view of security. Whereas the Sinai has at least a little territory to play with, which is not close to the populated centers of Israel, we had to deal with a situation in which both sides were negotiating every inch. The difficulties involved can be readily understood. There is some of that pattern here in this autonomy negotiation as well.

WILLIAM CRAWFORD, Islam Centennial 14: Could you expand on the question of European involvement—pros, cons, and the form it might take?

MR. SISCO: In the last ten days I have been in a number of discussions with Europeans who did start out some months ago with the idea of trying to amend Security Council Resolution 242. Although they have now arrived at a common approach toward a declaration, the declaration itself is still being negotiated. First, however, we should look at Europe in the broad strategic sense, because I don't think one ought to focus on the narrow tactical issues.

Europe obviously has a critical interest in this area, including the Persian Gulf, not only because a war might occur between the Israelis and the Arabs, but also because Europe must have continuing access to the oil resources of the Middle East. With the exception of Great Britain and Norway, Europe's dependence on that area is even greater than that of the United States.

The interest is there, but unfortunately—or fortunately as the case may be—this is not synonymous with the influence that the Europeans can exercise in this situation, for only the United States is acceptable to both sides. Furthermore, as a result of the special relationship that has existed and continues to exist, only the United States can bring about the necessary concessions, particularly vis-à-vis Israel.

Really, the role of the United States is central, whereas the Europeans—who understandably from a strategic, economic, and political point of view would like to see a resolution of the Arab-Israeli dispute and a peace settlement as the best guarantee of their particular interests—do not have the measure of influence that goes with it. For that reason, the injection of the European element many times tends to make the particular job of the United States even more difficult. Europe's basic position over the last ten or fifteen years has deviated somewhat from that of the United States, which has had to adopt a pragmatic approach.

Bringing two sides together in a negotiation requires great care. It entails not so much putting forward concrete ideas but rather trying to reconcile two sometimes irreconcilable points of view. In the case of the immediate European initiative, as long as it remains within the basic framework of the Camp David agreement, that kind of initiative will not have any far-reaching injurious effect on the efforts of the United States to achieve further progress in the autonomy accords themselves.

The important thing is this: in the Arab world, these declarations, while welcome, have been recognized for what they are, namely, statements of political support, but also a reflection of the inability of Europe to play a decisive and effective role in any negotiation between the two sides. Clearly, the perception in the Arab world is that although the Soviet Union can provide military assistance in any war effort, the three disengagement agreements and the Egyptian-Israeli Treaty indicate that only the United States can actually help make the peace.

HERMAN EDELSBERG, B'nai Brith International Council: Do the Europeans just want to go on record or do they really want a role in the mediation process?

MR. SISCO: For the moment, obviously they want mainly to record their position. Europe, or a number of Europeans, has been ambivalent, as you know. It has wanted a concrete role. Its biggest role to date was played behind the scenes by Britain at the time of the development of Security Council Resolution 242, but certainly between now and November Europe will limit itself to the declaratory approach. Remember that a special session of the UN General Assembly is scheduled to focus on the Palestinian issue in a few weeks.

Depending on what happens in the autonomy talks, after November we may see an attempt to develop a further instrumentality. Europe's prime objective, however, seems to be to create "a dialogue with the Arab world." Europe's ambivalence may reflect both a desire to ensure energy resources and Europe's recognition of its limited ability to affect negotiations between the Arabs and the Israelis.

HERBERT STEIN, American Enterprise Institute: You said that a common view in Israel is that the occupation of the West Bank should be ended, subject to the condition that the security of Israel should not be threatened. How do you reconcile these two differences?

MR. SISCO: Of course you could probably find a hundred different points of view on this question. An autonomy agreement would certainly be a practical test of peace on the ground in a very sensitive area. If it were in accord with Camp David, you would have a three-year interim period to demonstrate that Arabs and Israelis could in fact make autonomy work, and that would help to create a different atmosphere.

In the last two years of this interim accord, negotiations are supposed to pursue the critical issues of final borders, long-term security arrangements, the whole question of sovereignty, and the very key, Jerusalem, which all of us intended to set aside and put on the agenda as the last item. Clearly, from the Israeli point of view, some form of ongoing Israeli presence—military presence—will be required, and anything else probably will not prove politically feasible.

Now, I can imagine a situation in which the whole occupation status would be changed, political authority would come from the new autonomy instrumentality itself, and the governing council would provide solutions to the problems of water and land. Although we can envisage a short-run test of peace of that kind, I believe that any long-run solution has to be territorial. There has to be an actual division of territory whereby the Arabs are sovereign in whatever is given back and the Israelis are sovereign in whatever is retained. Autonomy is not the long-range solution to this problem.

CHRISTOPHER VAN HOLLEN, Carnegie Endowment for International Peace: Following up on that and looking beyond the five-year interim period, I wonder if you would elaborate on the West Bank–Jordanian possibility. This idea is favored by Peres, whereas others—such as George Ball, I believe—feel it is not viable. How do you see it?

MR. SISCO: Of all of the proposals developed and publicized over the years, I think that one possibly offers a positive prospect. First, there would be a division of territory. Second, even though Hussein is not part of the negotiating process, he does have an interest in the ultimate outcome and might be tempted to participate in a territorial approach, whereas he is not tempted by the current nonterritorial approach. Moreover, such an arrangement could be either federal—in other words, the West Bank would be an integral part of the state of Jordan—or it could be confederal, in order to give greater status to the West Bank under an overall umbrella of a Hashemite Kingdom of Jordon. That does not and should not preclude the possible ultimate exercise of a further act of self-determination.

The question of self-determination has to be viewed in terms of the environment, context, and time frame in which it takes place. At least theoretically, there is more apt to be an accommodation on a phased basis than the creation of some entity in one fell swoop. This is why autonomy can be considered a phase and why a territorial solution on a confederal basis can be considered a further phase. If that worked, the question of a separate entity would take on a completely different political possibility, on both sides, than it does today.

Obviously, this is an ideal evolutionary approach and only rose-colored glasses could make us believe that we have the time to apply it. Moreover, it would require that kind of leadership in the West Bank that is willing to risk such an operation. This is where Begin deserves a great deal of credit for making one specific decision that no other Israeli leader was willing or able to make: he told Sadat, in response to the Jerusalem visit, If you make peace with me I am willing to return the entire Sinai to Egyptian sovereignty. No other Israeli government has been able to make that decision or has had the power to make that decision.

At the same time, I am highly critical of Begin because of the settlements policy that he has pursued. If the principal threat to Israel is not military as long as Sadat remains in the peace framework, it must be a political threat. The erosion of public opinion in the United States and the erosion of public support in Western Europe, which has traditionally supported Israel, are key factors in the present situation. I believe that the settlements policy has contributed greatly to the erosion of support for Israel in this country and in Western Europe, which in the long run could have an adverse effect on the security of Israel itself. But I do not preclude this territorial approach at some point.

MR. VAN HOLLEN: Could you spell out the short-term hazards to Hussein in this type of formula?

MR. SISCO: Although the hazards are undeniably serious, they could prove manageable. Hussein's position today within the Arab brotherhood, which is probably as strong as it has been in the last two decades, in part has contributed to the strain in relationship between Jordan and the United States. In part, that strain has been caused by our mishandling of Hussein. Nonetheless, the hazards are manageable because even though Jordan may not have been part of the negotiating process, it has no interest in creating the kind of entity in the West Bank that could become attractive to the Palestinians in the East Bank. After all, there are 600,000 Palestinians in the East Bank, and the civil war is still fresh in Jordan's memory.

The most serious threat to the integrity of the king and Jordan was that civil war. It was initiated by the Palestinians and had the basic support of Syria. Despite the de facto accommodation, King Hussein cannot be naive enough to think that he is not in continuing danger from a political movement that would like to make both the West Bank and the East Bank separate unlinked Palestinian entities.

MR. GOLDWIN: You indicated that Hussein has no interest in establishing the kind of entity that could be an attraction to Palestinians on the East Bank. Do you mean a certain kind of independent Palestinian West Bank state, or do you mean any independent entity?

MR. SISCO: I was referring to a certain kind of independent state, and let me elaborate a bit. I would like to find the Palestinian leader, either in the West Bank or within the PLO—when and if he agrees to a negotiation based on 242 and based on a mutual recognition—who can say that he is the leader of the Palestinians and therefore can control all Palestinians.

Let us assume, for example, that Arafat as an element within the PLO is willing to apply a political solution—whatever that means. We have not gotten into that because regardless of the PLO's recent affirmation of support for a political solution, the basic covenant remains unchanged, so that what might sound good as a political solution may or may not make sense to both sides. Nonetheless, let us say hypothetically that the United States develops a negotiation—and whoever is in the White House in 1981 will have to make a major effort to break the back of the Arab-Israeli dispute and to resolve the Palestinian issue, regardless of the limitations between now and the end of 1980.

What leader, Arafat or anyone else, has sufficient strength to guarantee that he can keep the Palestinian movement within the peace process or peace framework? In other words, even if there is an eventual agreement based on a peaceful resolution of the problem and based on the concept of mutual recognition, can any Palestinian leader in the West Bank or within the PLO guarantee that unreconstructed elements would not continue to threaten Israel? And there are such elements within the PLO, in the radical wing of the Palestinian movement, that are still talking about and are still committed to the basic notion of a much broader Palestine, which would mean the demise of the state of Israel as we know it. To blink at this reality is utter naiveté. Thus, any Palestinian solution will have to be read very carefully. Furthermore, a political judgment will have to be made as to whether the leader involved can not only produce a solution on paper but can also assure its effective implementation.

Equally clear on the side of Israel, however, are some extremist Jewish elements in the West Bank, that are in part responsible for today's violence and counterviolence. I do not condone that any more than I do the extreme elements within the PLO movement or within the Arab world. Everything seems to depend on whether sufficient elements on both sides can reach an accommodation that is based on the principle of coexistence, and whether political leaders are strong enough to implement and to maintain it. That is a difficult question.

MR. GOLDWIN: What, then, does King Hussein want—an independent Palestinian state on the West Bank? Would that be in his interest?

MR. SISCO: Hussein's first preference is surely the creation of an entity in which he as a leader and the East Bank as part of the leadership have a decisive say. That would be his best protection. Otherwise, it would depend on the nature of the independent entity created. In any case, even if a moderate leadership were to create such an entity, without the significant political and economic involvement of Hussein and the East Bank of the Jordan, the situation would become a threat to both Jordan and Israel. That is my view, which is not conventional wisdom, by the way.

JUDITH KIPPER, American Enterprise Institute: Would you explain mutual recognition further? If it is based on 242 as it now stands, the Israelis have recognized that some Palestinians have the status of refugees and that there is a refugee problem. Who, then, on the Palestinian side ought to recognize Israel?

We are talking about Palestinian leaders, and seeking leadership on the West Bank. Two mayors have been blown up in the past two weeks. Two other mayors visiting Washington recently have been speaking everywhere—even in a synagogue, which was a rather large event here—about recognition, saying over and over again that they are a poor Palestinian state living side by side with Israel. They did, by the way, for the first time have the privilege of meeting a senior official at the State Department. Where, then, does mutual recognition come from if in fact there is no national right? Which Palestinians should recognize Israel's national right when Israel has already recognized the refugee question?

Mr. Sisco: You have raised four or five good questions, but I am not sure that there are easy answers to any of them. As far as 242 is concerned, the refugee question at that time was considered primarily in the nonpolitical context. Therefore 242 says nothing about the political aspect of the Palestinian problem.

When I use the term "recognition," it, to me, means different things at different times. By 1981 the critical question will be, Who will be the participants in any negotiation? That is part of the negotiation itself. In other words, the question of participants may be seen from one quarter as a procedural issue, whereas Israel certainly does not consider this to be a procedural issue, but a totally substantive issue. Thus, recognition entails a decision on who the participants will be. Here, I have long been of the view that there won't be a meaningful negotiation if it rests on the present formula—namely, that the PLO should be "the sole representative." That will not be a politically feasible formula in the coming years.

In certain circumstances, PLO representatives might be part of the Palestinian, Jordanian, or Arab representation. There are various possibilities here. In the first stage, however, we will probably not see a strictly PLO negotiation. Much of the groundwork has to be done behind the scenes. That is, the question of participation will have to be tied in with the objectives of the substantive negotiations. Resolution 242 does not exclude the Palestinians—after all, the principal focus of 242 as well as of 338 was negotiation between the two sides. Furthermore, the Palestinians were not excluded in the second part of Camp David. The phrase "Palestinian Arabs" is used. Thus at some distant point Palestinians of various stripes, including certain elements from the PLO, might be included.

Emile Nakhleh, American Enterprise Institute: The first part of your comments seemed to pinpoint the crux of the problem, namely, how to get the negotiations started, with the participation of the proper parties—that is, the Jordanians and the Palestinians—in addition to the parties that are currently involved. I support your statements that any solution must be territorial, which means in your analysis here the end of occupation as a system (that does not preclude the presence of Israeli soldiers for security arrangements) and a recognition of the ultimate principle of sovereignty over that territory. Our research in the area indicates that these are the two basic requirements that the Palestinians have raised in order for them to participate in the negotiations. The question is, Who is going to make this statement?

The Jordanians and the Palestinians as one delegation would most likely participate once these two principles are recognized. Yet you indicate that Mr. Begin is not likely to accept territorial solutions or to leave the scene in the foreseeable future. That means for the next twelve months or so we will not see any movement. What impact would the failure to get the process going have on the moderate elements in the region?

The second part of your comments, with due respect, appear to be tangential to the problem that we are concerned with. They focus on a priori legislation of a responsible state. I think that is too far in the future. My concern is to involve the Palestinians in the negotiating process.

MR. SISCO: On your second point, it is too early for an explicit agreement, but a political judgment has to be made about ultimate goals. With or without the kind of limited autonomy agreement that I described, the United States will have to be the initiator, and will have to develop ideas that address this issue procedurally as well as substantively. By substantively, I mean substantive framework as well as a method of bringing the various groups into the process.

These issues could be focused on in the first few months of 1981 if the present administration were to continue. I do not want my remarks to be interpreted as partisan in any sense of the word, but the point is that a new administration obviously will take longer to become educated to the realities. I wish that some major movement were possible sooner. People who want to address the Palestinian issue in a fundamental sense at this time do not understand —or at least are disregarding—the political realities.

The so-called moderate elements in the Arab world are quite sophisticated and understand very well our process and its limitations. Because we have faced the Palestinian issue for a number of years, some might say that it is not solvable. I do not believe that key leaders in the area or in the United States take this particular attitude. The United States obviously could not afford to think that way because diplomacy requires an element of measured optimism in order for it to operate.

No country other than the United States can put together this basic framework. It is significant that the autonomy talks will resume in the next week or two as a result of whatever ideas the United States puts forward. There's just no substitute. Now I am not suggesting that a new peace plan will be launched in early 1981, but only that such a framework has to be developed and negotiated in time by the

United States. The administration has officially stated that if Security Council Resolution 242 and/or Israel's right to exist were accepted, it would reconsider U.S. policy on the Palestinian issue. That framework has been established.

Moreover, we tend to denigrate the advance represented by Camp David and the phrase, the "rights of the Palestinians," that appears there, but this goes well beyond the pronouncements of several years ago that mentioned only "legitimate interests and aspirations" of the Palestinians.

Although both sides in the dispute have a different interpretation of that phrase, it is significant that 242 permitted the negotiation of the Egyptian-Israeli Treaty and that the second half of Camp David is a formula of sufficient ambiguity and broadness to allow, as did 242, different interpretations by both sides. Such phrases are given concreteness by the actual negotiation, but it is the United States that will have to bring them to the negotiation, both procedurally and substantively.

DAVID BRODY, Anti-Defamation League: If there is a new administration, apart from any delay because of its unfamiliarity with the problems—a delay that would be reduced considerably if a Mr. Sisco were a part of that new administration—would there be any major change in the ongoing autonomy talks and in the progress of peace in the Middle East?

MR. SISCO: That question can be answered in two ways. If we assume a continuation of the Carter administration, we have to take into account the Camp David accord and the short-run objective of achieving an autonomy agreement. Let's assume for a moment that they really achieve this limited success—a little piece of paper that says that Egypt and Israel agree on some sort of autonomy arrangement. At such a point, no Palestinians or Jordanians are participating. With or without such an autonomy agreement, by 1981 a fresh territorial approach to the West Bank and Gaza will be required.

Second, I believe that substantive talks on the Syrian-Israeli aspect will have to be opened as well. I do not mean that a huge peace conference is needed, but that we must begin to address the issue across the board.

A new administration, on one hand, would not be tied to past objectives such as autonomy in the same way as the ongoing administration. But basically, the same evaluation will have to be made: Do you shift the approach, or do you stay with the basic framework?

I suspect that it's going to be necessary to make some major shifts in the approach. Even in a major shift of approach, autonomy within a broad kind of framework can still be a phased part of the process, if it is useful. Thus we might begin to negotiate on the basis of a territorial division that would follow a period of evolving autonomy. We cannot really predict how this is going to be played. What is clear is that at the end of the line a territorial solution will be required in relation to the West Bank and the Gaza as well as the Syrian-Israeli border.

MURRAY WEIDENBAUM, American Enterprise Institute: What would be the future role of the West Bank mayors? Are there any circumstances under which they might have any diplomatic role?

MR. SISCO: My concern is this: Present developments are forcing them to take a political position that is no different from that of some PLO leaders. In other words, a process of radicalization is going on that is of some concern.

We should recall that when Israel conducted elections in the West Bank in 1976, the PLO announced publicly that it was absolutely opposed to these elections. Privately, however, it suggested that Palestinian leaders in the West Bank run for these offices because of their potential importance. Those two unfortunate victims who were blown up were the very mayors who decided to run for office so that they could influence the situation more effectively from public office than by means of boycotting.

Now, those mayors were the hope and continue to be the hope, insofar as autonomy talks are concerned. If radicalization continues, however, there really will not be many such leaders around in the West Bank, and that will complicate the problem even further. Although radicalization appears to be continuing, I do not think that by the time we focus on this in a serious way eight to twelve months from now that there will not be someone with whom to negotiate. I think that the reality is that as long as the underlying military balance is maintained, the radicals are not going to be able to achieve their objectives by war.

CHARLES FAIRBANKS, American Enterprise Institute: Recent discussions in the part of the American community that is concerned with this issue have focused on the possibility of putting pressure on Israel to make greater concessions, first in the autonomy talks, and later, toward the Palestinian state. Now, it is always the case in diplomacy, where one power has influence over another power, that pressure to achieve certain things is constructive when those things can be achieved, while pressure to achieve certain other things is counterproductive when they can't be achieved, and one simply sacrifices one's influence under those circumstances. Could you differentiate between these two categories—things that the United States might fruitfully exert pressure on Israel to do, and things in which the United States just throws away its influence, if it tries to persuade Israel to do them?

MR. SISCO: That is very difficult to do. First, we have to recognize the basic asymmetry of the situation in the sense that we do have a special relationship with Israel. The Arab world views this relationship in terms of what sort of concessions the United States can bring about vis-à-vis Israel. I assume that concessions will be required on both sides, and that is why I have focused on the kind of commitments that any Palestinian leader or leaders must be able to make and to implement effectively if a serious negotiation with a serious result is ultimately to be achieved. It is not enough merely to recognize Israel's right to exist. What is behind it? Can a Palestinian leader make an agreement stick? Can he be an effective leader who controls the Palestinians and causes them to abide by agreements? This is not an unreasonable question for Israelis to ask.

Commitments from Arab states could be introduced in order to create some sort of symmetry of commitments, but the United States should not really make such distinctions in various issues or categories. Our role as the central catalytic agent should remain a pragmatic one. The greatest danger would be for the United States to come out prematurely with a substantive plan of its own that would satisfy neither side but that would merely draw the focus of ire on us and would undermine our particular role as the negotiator. The old truism still holds, that this is a negotiation between the two sides in the Middle East and that we should not become a substitute for the two principal negotiators. We must remember the people who have to live with the results of the peace.

Certainly we are intimately involved because of the area's overwhelming strategic interest. Historically, we have also been committed to the security and the survival of Israel. The second prong of our policy has been and continues to be access to the oil resources of the Middle East in addition to doing whatever is necessary to avoid a potential confrontation over this strategic area between ourselves and the Soviet Union. So we have some overriding interests in this situation.

I believe that we can play a role of guarantor of peace. We must not take the word "guarantor" too literally, however; the word is used erroneously by some who want to substitute the United States as a guarantor for the concessions that are going to have to be made by both sides. I don't mean that—I mean the continuing involvement of the United States in this area by way of assistance and by way of its position as a supplement to a peace agreement, which contains the principal assurances, commitments, and guarantees between the principal parties themselves.

Here, you've got to understand the Arab-Israeli dispute in the larger context. The lesson of Afghanistan is severalfold. If the United States is going to become vulnerable—that is, in terms of strategic nuclear deterrence—in the early 1980s, we must do everything possible over the next three to five years to safeguard against this vulnerability. If the Soviet Union, knowing that we had no conventional option in the area of the Persian Gulf and that we were preoccupied with Iran, did not miscalculate in Afghanistan, then the number one priority for the United States is to restore the credibility and the integrity of American power—and this cannot be divorced from the Middle East and the Persian Gulf—and to create the kind of conventional option and capacity for quick response in the area of the Persian Gulf that is a meaningful option.

I am not suggesting for a moment gunboat diplomacy or the substitution of military power for the resolution of the political, economic, and social problems of the Third World. I am certainly not suggesting that a fleet of American aircraft carriers could resolve any instability that might develop in Saudi Arabia. That presence is important, however, as a manifestation of the American political commitment to our friends in the area—including Saudi Arabia, King Hussein, Israel, and Egypt—and as an indication that the United States considers this area absolutely vital to its interests and to the interests of the free world. That will have a direct impact on the centrality of our role in the Arab-Israeli dispute, as it will on the continuing achievement of our overall political, economic, and strategic interests in this area, including not only the security and survival of Israel, but also direct access to the oil resources of the Middle East and the Persian Gulf.

As a result, we cannot really divorce these regional problems from the general global position of the United States. One reason for our uncertain image abroad in recent years is that we have allowed our prestige to continue to slide and therefore we have confounded both our friends and our adversaries. Whoever is in the White House in 1981 will have to come to grips with this problem.

MR. GOLDWIN: Thank you very much, Dr. Sisco.

Appendix A

Text of the Camp David Agreements, Signed September 17, 1978, and UN Security Council Resolutions 242 and 338

A Framework for Peace in the Middle East Agreed at Camp David

Muhammad Anwar al-Sadat, President of the Arab Republic of Egypt, and Menachem Begin, Prime Minister of Israel, met with Jimmy Carter, President of the United States of America, at Camp David from September 5 to September 17, 1978, and have agreed on the following framework for peace in the Middle East. They invite other parties to the Arab-Israeli conflict to adhere to it.

Preamble

The search for peace in the Middle East must be guided by the following:

—The agreed basis for a peaceful settlement of the conflict between Israel and its neighbors is United Nations Security Council Resolution 242, in all its parts.*

—After four wars during thirty years, despite intensive human efforts, the Middle East, which is the cradle of civilization and the birthplace of three great religions, does not yet enjoy the blessings of peace. The people of the Middle East yearn for peace so that the vast human and natural resources of the region can be turned to the pursuits of peace and so that this area can become a model for coexistence and cooperation among nations.

—The historic initiative of President Sadat in visiting Jerusalem and the reception accorded to him by the Parliament, government and

*The texts of Resolutions 242 and 338 are annexed to this document.

people of Israel, and the reciprocal visit of Prime Minister Begin to Ismailia, the peace proposals made by both leaders, as well as the warm reception of these missions by the peoples of both countries, have created an unprecedented opportunity for peace which must not be lost if this generation and future generations are to be spared the tragedies of war.

—The provisions of the Charter of the United Nations and the other accepted norms of international law and legitimacy now provide accepted standards for the conduct of relations among all states.

—To achieve a relationship of peace, in the spirit of Article 2 of the United Nations Charter, future negotiations between Israel and any neighbor prepared to negotiate peace and security with it, are necessary for the purpose of carrying out all the provisions and principles of Resolutions 242 and 338.

—Peace requires respect for the sovereignty, territorial integrity and political independence of every state in the area and their right to live in peace within secure and recognized boundaries free from threats or acts of force. Progress toward that goal can accelerate movement toward a new era of reconciliation in the Middle East marked by cooperation in promoting economic development, in maintaining stability, and in assuring security.

—Security is enhanced by a relationship of peace and by cooperation between nations which enjoy normal relations. In addition, under the terms of peace treaties, the parties can, on the basis of reciprocity, agree to special security arrangements such as demilitarized zones, limited armaments areas, early warning stations, the presence of international forces, liaison, agreed measures for monitoring, and other arrangements that they agree are useful.

Framework

Taking these factors into account, the parties are determined to reach a just, comprehensive, and durable settlement of the Middle East conflict through the conclusion of peace treaties based on Security Council Resolutions 242 and 338 in all their parts. Their purpose is to achieve peace and good neighborly relations. They recognize that, for peace to endure, it must involve all those who have been most deeply affected by the conflict. They therefore agree that this framework as appropriate is intended by them to constitute a basis for peace not only between Egypt and Israel, but also between Israel and each of its other neighbors which is prepared to negotiate peace with Israel on this basis. With that objective in mind, they have agreed to proceed as follows:

A. *West Bank and Gaza*

1. Egypt, Israel, Jordan and the representatives of the Palestinian people should participate in negotiations on the resolution of the Palestinian problem in all its aspects. To achieve that objective, nego-

tiations relating to the West Bank and Gaza should proceed in three stages:

(a) Egypt and Israel agree that, in order to ensure a peaceful and orderly transfer of authority, and taking into account the security concerns of all the parties, there should be transitional arrangements for the West Bank and Gaza for a period not exceeding five years. In order to provide full autonomy to the inhabitants, under these arrangements the Israeli military government and its civilian administration will be withdrawn as soon as a self-governing authority has been freely elected by the inhabitants of these areas to replace the existing military government. To negotiate the details of a transitional arrangement, the Government of Jordan will be invited to join the negotiations on the basis of this framework. These new arrangements should give due consideration both to the principle of self-government by the inhabitants of these territories and to the legitimate security concerns of the parties involved.

(b) Egypt, Israel, and Jordan will agree on the modalities for establishing the elected self-governing authority in the West Bank and Gaza. The delegations of Egypt and Jordan may include Palestinians from the West Bank and Gaza or other Palestinians as mutually agreed. The parties will negotiate an agreement which will define the powers and responsibilities of the self-governing authority to be exercised in the West Bank and Gaza. A withdrawal of Israeli armed forces will take place and there will be a redeployment of the remaining Israeli forces into specified security locations. The agreement will also include arrangements for assuring internal and external security and public order. A strong local police force will be established, which may include Jordanian citizens. In addition, Israel and Jordanian forces will participate in joint patrols and in the manning of control posts to assure the security of the borders.

(c) When the self-governing authority (administrative council) in the West Bank and Gaza is established and inaugurated, the transitional period of five years will begin. As soon as possible, but not later than the third year after the beginning of the transitional period, negotiations will take place to determine the final status of the West Bank and Gaza and its relationship with its neighbors, and to conclude a peace treaty between Israel and Jordan by the end of the transitional period. These negotiations will be conducted among Egypt, Israel, Jordan, and the elected representatives of the inhabitants of the West Bank and Gaza. Two separate but related committees will be convened, one committee, consisting of representatives of the four parties which will negotiate and agree on the final status of the West Bank and Gaza, and its relationship with its neighbors, and the second committee, consisting of representatives of Israel and representatives of Jordan to be joined by the elected representatives of the inhabitants of the West Bank and Gaza, to negotiate the peace treaty between

Israel and Jordan, taking into account the agreement reached on the final status of the West Bank and Gaza. The negotiations shall be based on all the provisions and principles of UN Security Council Resolution 242. The negotiations will resolve, among other matters, the location of the boundaries and the nature of the security arrangements. The solution from the negotiations must also recognize the legitimate rights of the Palestinian people and their just requirements. In this way, the Palestinians will participate in the determination of their own future through:

1) The negotiations among Egypt, Israel, Jordan and the representatives of the inhabitants of the West Bank and Gaza to agree on the final status of the West Bank and Gaza and other outstanding issues by the end of the transitional period.

2) Submitting their agreement to a vote by the elected representatives of the inhabitants of the West Bank and Gaza.

3) Providing for the elected representatives of the inhabitants of the West Bank and Gaza to decide how they shall govern themselves consistent with the provisions of their agreement.

4) Participating as stated above in the work of the committee negotiating the peace treaty between Israel and Jordan.

2. All necessary measures will be taken and provisions made to assure the security of Israel and its neighbors during the transitional period and beyond. To assist in providing such security, a strong local police force will be constituted by the self-governing authority. It will be composed of inhabitants of the West Bank and Gaza. The police will maintain continuing liaison on internal security matters with the designated Israeli, Jordanian, and Egyptian officers.

3. During the transitional period, representatives of Egypt, Israel, Jordan, and the self-governing aurthority will constitute a continuing committee to decide by agreement on the modalities of admission of persons displaced from the West Bank and Gaza in 1967, together with necessary measures to prevent disruption and disorder. Other matters of common concern may also be dealt with by this committee.

4. Egypt and Israel will work with each other and with other interested parties to establish agreed procedures for a prompt, just and permanent implementation of the resolution of the refugee problem.

B. *Egypt-Israel*

1. Egypt and Israel undertake not to resort to the threat or the use of force to settle disputes. Any disputes shall be settled by peaceful means in accordance with the provisions of Article 33 of the Charter of the United Nations.

2. In order to achieve peace between them, the parties agree to negotiate in good faith with a goal of concluding within three months from the signing of this Framework a peace treaty between them,

while inviting the other parties to the conflict to proceed simultaneously to negotiate and conclude similar peace treaties with a view to achieving a comprehensive peace in the area. The Framework for the Conclusion of a Peace Treaty between Egypt and Israel will govern the peace negotiations between them. The parties will agree on the modalities and the timetable for the implementation of their obligations under the treaty.

C. *Associated Principles*

1. Egypt and Israel state that the principles and provisions described below should apply to peace treaties between Israel and each of its neighbors—Egypt, Jordan, Syria and Lebanon.

2. Signatories shall establish among themselves relationships normal to states at peace with one another. To this end, they should undertake to abide by all the provisions of the Charter of the United Nations. Steps to be taken in this respect include:

(a) full recognition;

(b) abolishing economic boycotts;

(c) guaranteeing that under their jurisdiction the citizens of the other parties shall enjoy the protection of the due process of law.

3. Signatories should explore possibilities for economic development in the context of final peace treaties, with the objective of contributing to the atmosphere of peace, cooperation and friendship which is their common goal.

4. Claims Commissions may be established for the mutual settlement of all financial claims.

5. The United States shall be invited to participate in the talks on matters related to the modalities of the implementation of the agreements and working out the timetable for the carrying out of the obligations of the parties.

6. The United Nations Security Council shall be requested to endorse the peace treaties and ensure that their provisions shall not be violated. The permanent members of the Security Council shall be requested to underwrite the peace treaties and ensure respect for their provisions. They shall also be requested to conform their policies and actions with the undertakings contained in this Framework.

For the Government of the Arab Republic of Egypt:	For the Government of Israel:
A. SADAT	M. BEGIN

Witnessed by:

JIMMY CARTER

Jimmy Carter, President
of the United States of America

Annex

Text of United Nations Security Council Resolution 242 of November 22, 1967

Adopted unanimously at the 1382nd meeting

The Security Council,

Expressing its continuing concern with the grave situation in the Middle East,

Emphasizing the inadmissibility of the acquisition of territory by war and the need to work for a just and lasting peace in which every State in the area can live in security,

Emphasizing further that all Member States in their acceptance of the Charter of the United Nations have undertaken a commitment to act in accordance with Article 2 of the Charter,

1. *Affirms* that the fulfilment of Charter principles requires the establishment of a just and lasting peace in the Middle East which should include the application of both the following principles:

(i) Withdrawal of Israeli armed forces from territories occupied in the recent conflict;

(ii) Termination of all claims or states of belligerency and respect for and acknowledgement of the sovereignty, territorial integrity and political independence of every State in the area and their right to live in peace within secure and recognized boundaries free from threats or acts of force;

2. *Affirms further* the necessity

(a) For guaranteeing freedom of navigation through international waterways in the area;

(b) For achieving a just settlement of the refugee problem;

(c) For guaranteeing the territorial inviolability and political independence of every State in the area, through measures including the establishment of demilitarized zones;

3. *Requests* the Secretary-General to designate a Special Representative to proceed to the Middle East to establish and maintain contacts with the States concerned in order to promote agreement and assist efforts to achieve a peaceful and accepted settlement in accordance with the provisions and principles of this resolution.

4. *Requests* the Secretary-General to report to the Security Council on the progress of the efforts of the Special Representative as soon as possible.

Text of United Nations Security Council Resolution 338

Adopted by the Security Council at its 1747th meeting, on 21/22 October 1973

The Security Council

1. *Calls upon* all parties to the present fighting to cease all firing and terminate all military activity immediately, no later than 12 hours

after the moment of the adoption of this decision, in the positions they now occupy;

2. *Calls upon* the parties concerned to start immediately after the cease-fire the implementation of Security Council Resolution 242 (1967) in all of its parts;

3. *Decides* that, immediately and concurrently with the cease-fire, negotiations start between the parties concerned under appropriate auspices aimed at establishing a just and durable peace in the Middle East.

Framework for the Conclusion of a Peace Treaty between Egypt and Israel

In order to achieve peace between them, Israel and Egypt agree to negotiate in good faith with a goal of concluding within three months of the signing of this framework a peace treaty between them.

It is agreed that:

The site of the negotiations will be under a United Nations flag at a location or locations to be mutually agreed.

All of the principles of U.N. Resolution 242 will apply in this resolution of the dispute between Israel and Egypt.

Unless otherwise mutually agreed, terms of the peace treaty will be implemented between two and three years after the peace treaty is signed.

The following matters are agreed between the parties:

(a) the full exercise of Egyptian sovereignty up to the internationally recognized border between Egypt and mandated Palestine;

(b) the withdrawal of Israeli armed forces from the Sinai;

(c) the use of airfields left by the Israelis near El Arish, Rafah, Ras en Naqb, and Sharm el Sheikh for civilian purposes only, including possible commercial use by all nations;

(d) the right of free passage by ships of Israel through the Gulf of Suez and the Suez Canal on the basis of the Constantinople Convention of 1888 applying to all nations; the Strait of Tiran and the Gulf of Aqaba are international waterways to be open to all nations for unimpeded and nonsuspendable freedom of navigation and overflight;

(e) the construction of a highway between the Sinai and Jordan near Elat with guaranteed free and peaceful passage by Egypt and Jordan; and

(f) the stationing of military forces listed below.

Stationing of Forces

A. No more than one division (mechanized or infantry) of Egyptian armed forces will be stationed within an area lying approximately 50 kilometers (km) east of the Gulf of Suez and the Suez Canal.

B. Only United Nations forces and civil police equipped with light weapons to perform normal police functions will be stationed within an area lying west of the international border and the Gulf of Aqaba, varying in width from 20 km to 40 km.

C. In the area within 3 km east of the international border there will be Israeli limited military forces not to exceed four infantry battalions and United Nations observers.

D. Border patrol units, not to exceed three battalions, will supplement the civil police in maintaining order in the area not included above.

The exact demarcation of the above areas will be as decided during the peace negotiations.

Early warning stations may exist to insure compliance with the terms of the agreement.

United Nations forces will be stationed: (a) in part of the area in the Sinai lying within about 20 km of the Mediterranean Sea and adjacent to the international border, and (b) in the Sharm el Sheikh area to ensure freedom of passage through the Strait of Tiran; and these forces will not be removed unless such removal is approved by the Security Council of the United Nations with a unanimous vote of the five permanent members.

After a peace treaty is signed, and after the interim withdrawal is complete, normal relations will be established between Egypt and Israel, including: full recognition, including diplomatic, economic and cultural relations; termination of economic boycotts and barriers to the free movement of goods and people; and mutual protection of citizens by the due process of law.

Interim Withdrawal

Between three months and nine months after the signing of the peace treaty, all Israeli forces will withdraw east of a line extending from a point east to El Arish to Ras Muhammad, the exact location of this line to be determined by mutual agreement.

For the Government of the Arab Republic of Egypt:	For the Government of Israel:
A. Sadat	M. Begin

Witnessed by:

Jimmy Carter

Jimmy Carter, President
of the United States of America

Appendix B

The Palestinian National Covenant July 17, 1968

The Palestinian National Covenant
This Covenant will be called "The Palestinian National Covenant" (Al-Mithaq Al-Watani Al-Filastini).

Articles of the Covenant
Article 1) Palestine is the homeland of the Palestinian Arab people and an integral part of the great Arab homeland, and the people of Palestine is a part of the Arab nation.

Article 2) Palestine with its boundaries that existed at the time of the British mandate is an integral regional unit.

Article 3) The Palestinian Arab people possesses the legal right to its homeland, and when the liberation of its homeland is completed it will exercise self-determination solely according to its own will and choice.

Article 4) The Palestinian personality is an innate, persistent characteristic that does not disappear, and it is transferred from fathers to sons. The Zionist occupation, and the dispersal of the Palestinian Arab people as a result of the disasters which came over it, do not deprive it of its Palestinian personality and affiliation and do not nullify them.

Article 5) The Palestinians are the Arab citizens who were living permanently in Palestine until 1947, whether they were expelled from there or remained. Whoever is born to a Palestinian Arab father after this date, within Palestine or outside it, is a Palestinian.

Article 6) Jews who were living permanently in Palestine until the beginning of the Zionist invasion will be considered Palestinians.

NOTE: Text of the Palestinian National Covenant as of May 1978.

Article 7) The Palestinian affiliation and the material, spiritual and historical tie with Palestine are permanent realities. The upbringing of the Palestinian individual in an Arab and revolutionary fashion, the undertaking of all means of forging consciousness and training the Palestinian, in order to acquaint him profoundly with his homeland, spiritually and materially, and preparing him for the conflict and the armed struggle, as well as for the sacrifice of his property and his life to restore his homeland, until the liberation—all this is a national duty.

Article 8) The phase in which the people of Palestine is living is that of the national (*Watani*) struggle for the liberation of Palestine. Therefore, the contradictions among the Palestinian national forces are of a secondary order which must be suspended in the interest of the fundamental contradiction between Zionism and Colonialism on the one side and the Palestinian Arab people on the other. On this basis, the Palestinian masses, whether in the homeland or in places of exile (*Mahajir*), organizations and individuals, comprise one national front which acts to restore Palestine and liberate it through armed struggle.

Article 9) Armed struggle is the only way to liberate Palestine and is therefore a strategy and not tactics. The Palestinian Arab people affirms its absolute resolution and abiding determination to pursue the armed struggle and to march forward toward the armed popular revolution, to liberate its homeland and return it (to maintain) its right to a natural life in it, and to exercise its right of self-determination in it and sovereignty over it.

Article 10) Fedayeen action forms the nucleus of the popular Palestinian War of Liberation. This demands its promotion, extension and protection, and the mobilization of all the mass and scientific capacities of the Palestinians, their organization and involvement in the armed Palestinian revolution, and cohesion in the national (*Watani*) struggle among the various groups of the people of Palestine, and between them and the Arab masses, to guarantee the continuation of the revolution, its advancement and victory.

Article 11) The Palestinians will have three mottoes: National (*Wataniyya*) unity, national (*Qawmiyya*) mobilization and liberation.

Article 12) The Palestinian Arab people believes in Arab unity. In order to fulfill its role in realizing this, it must preserve, in this phase of its national (*Watani*) struggle, its Palestinian personality and the constituents thereof, increase consciousness of its existence and resist any plan that tends to disintegrate or weaken it.

Article 13) Arab unity and the Liberation of Palestine are two complementary aims. Each one paves the way for realization of the other. Arab unity leads to the Liberation of Palestine, and the Liberation of Palestine leads to Arab unity. Working for both goes hand in hand.

Article 14) The destiny of the Arab nation, indeed the very Arab existence, depends upon the destiny of the Palestine issue. The endeavor and effort of the Arab nation to liberate Palestine follows from this connection. The people of Palestine assumes its vanguard role in realizing this sacred national (*Qawmi*) aim.

Article 15) The liberation of Palestine, from an Arab viewpoint, is a national (*Qawmi*) duty to repulse the Zionist, Imperalist invasion from the great Arab homeland and to purge the Zionist presence from Palestine. Its full responsibilities fall upon the Arab nation, peoples and governments, with the Palestinian Arab people at their head.

For this purpose, the Arab nation must mobilize all its military, human, material and spiritual capacities to participate actively with the people of Palestine in the liberation of Palestine. They must, especially in the present stage of armed Palestinian revolution, grant and offer the people of Palestine all possible help and every material and human support, and afford it every sure means and opportunity enabling it to continue to assume its vanguard role in pursuing its armed revolution until the liberation of its homeland.

Article 16) The liberation of Palestine, from a spiritual viewpoint, will prepare an atmosphere of tranquility and peace for the Holy Land, in the shade of which all the holy places will be safeguarded, and freedom of worship and visitation to all will be guaranteed without distinction or discrimination of race, color, language or religion. For this reason, the people of Palestine looks to the support of all the spiritual forces in the world.

Article 17) The liberation of Palestine, from a human viewpoint, will restore to the Palestinian man his dignity, glory and freedom. For this, the Palestinian Arab people looks to the support of those in the world who believe in the dignity and freedom of man.

Article 18) The liberation of Palestine, from an international viewpoint, is a defensive act necessitated by the requirements of self-defense. For this reason, the people of Palestine, desiring to befriend all peoples, looks to the support of the states which love freedom, justice and peace in restoring the legal situation to Palestine, establishing security and peace in its territory, and enabling its people to exercise national (*Wataniyya*) sovereignty and national (*Qawmiyya*) freedom.

Article 19) The partitioning of Palestine in 1947 and the establishment of Israel is fundamentally null and void, whatever time has elapsed, because it was contrary to the wish of the people of Palestine and its natural right to its homeland, and contradicts the principles embodied in the Charter of the United Nations, the first of which is the right of self-determination.

Article 20) The Balfour Declaration, the mandate document, and what has been based upon them are considered null and void. The claim of a historical or spiritual tie between Jews and Palestine does not tally with historical realities nor with the constituents of statehood in their true sense. Judaism, in its character as a religion of revelation, is not a nationality with an independent existence. Likewise, the Jews are not one people with an independent personality. They are rather citizens of the states to which they belong.

Article 21) The Palestinian Arab people, in expressing itself through the armed Palestinian Revolution, rejects every solution that is a substitute for a complete liberation of Palestine and rejects all plans that aim at the settlement of the Palestine issue or its internationalization.

Article 22) Zionism is a political movement organically related to world imperialism and hostile to all movements of liberation and progress in the world. It is a racist and fanatical movement in its formation; aggressive, expansionist and colonialist in its aims; and Fascist and Nazi in its means. Israel is the tool of the Zionist movement and a human and geographical base for world imperialism. It is a concentration and jumping-off point for imperialism in the heart of the Arab homeland, to strike at the hopes of the Arab nation for liberation, unity and progress.

Israel is a constant threat to peace in the Middle East and the entire world. Since the liberation of Palestine will liquidate the Zionist and Imperialist presence and bring about the stabilization of peace in the Middle East, the people of Palestine looks to the support of all liberal men of the world and all the forces of good, progress and peace; and implores all of them, regardless of their different leanings and orientations, to offer all help and support to the people of Palestine in its just and legal struggle to liberate its homeland.

Article 23) The demands of security and peace and the requirements of truth and justice oblige all states that preserve friendly relations among peoples and maintain the loyalty of citizens to their homelands to consider Zionism an illegitimate movement and to prohibit its existence and activity.

Article 24) The Palestinian Arab people believes in the principles of justice, freedom, sovereignty, self-determination, human dignity and the right of peoples to exercise them.

Article 25) To realize the aims of this covenant and its principles the Palestine Liberation Organization will undertake its full role in liberating Palestine.

Article 26) The Palestine Liberation Organization, which represents the forces of the Palestinian revolution, is responsible for the movement of the Palestinian Arab people in its struggle to restore its homeland, liberate it, return to it and exercise the right of self-determination in it. This responsibility extends to all military, political and financial matters, and all else that the Palestine issue requires in the Arab and international spheres.

Article 27) The Palestine Liberation Organization will cooperate with all Arab states, each according to its capacities, and will maintain neutrality in their mutual relations in the light of and on the basis of, the requirements of the Battle of Liberation, and will not interfere in the internal affairs of any Arab State.

Article 28) The Palestinian Arab people insists upon the originality and independence of its national (*Wataniyya*) revolution and rejects every manner of interference, guardianship and subordination.

Article 29) The Palestinian Arab people possesses the prior and original right in liberating and restoring its homeland and will define its positions with reference to the issue (of Palestine) and the extent of their support for (the Palestinian Arab people) in its revolution to realize its aims.

Article 30) The fighters and bearers of arms in the Battle of Liberation are the nucleus of the Popular Army, which will be the protecting arm of the gains of the Palestinian Arab people.

Article 31) This organization shall have a flag, oath and anthem, all of which will be determined in accordance with a special system.

Article 32) To this covenant is attached a law known as the fundamental law of the Palestine Liberation Organization, in which is determined the manner of the organization's formation, its committees, institutions, the special functions of every one of them and all the requisite duties associated with them in accordance with this covenant.

Article 33) This Covenant cannot be amended except by a two-thirds majority of all the members of the National Council of the Palestine Liberation Organization in a special session called for this purpose.